PAUL BUNYAN AND BABE THE BLUE OX

Copyright © 1991 Steck-Vaughn Company

Copyright © 1985, Raintree Publishers Limited Partnership
All rights reserved. No part of the material protected by this
copyright may be reproduced or utilized in any form by any
means, electronic or mechanical, including photocopying,
recording, or by any information storage and retrieval system,
without permission in writing from the copyright owner.
Requests for permission to make copies of any part of the work
should be mailed to: Copyright Permissions, Steck-Vaughn
Company, P.O. Box 26015, Austin, TX 78755. Printed in the
United States of America.

5 6 7 8 9 10 11   98 97 96 95 94 93 92

Library of Congress Number: 84-9786

Library of Congress Cataloging in Publication Data

Gleiter, Jan, 1947-
    Paul Bunyan and Babe the blue ox.

    Summary: Tall tales of the mighty logger, including his
birth and his adventures in a logging camp, in the South
Dakota forests, and among the California redwoods.

    1. Bunyan, Paul, (Legendary character)—Juvenile
literature. [1. Bunyan, Paul (Legendary character)
2. Folklore—United States.   3. Tall tales]   I. Thompson,
Kathleen.   II. Miyake, Yoshi, ill.   III. Title.
PZ8.1.G4595Pau   1984   398.2′2′0973   84-9786
ISBN 0-8172-2119-0 lib. bdg.
ISBN 0-8172-2262-2 softcover

PAUL BUNYAN AND BABE THE BLUE OX

Jan Gleiter and Kathleen Thompson
Illustrated by Yoshi Miyake

RAINTREE
STECK-VAUGHN
L I B R A R Y
A Division of Steck-Vaughn Company

Paul Bunyan was big. That's the first thing that anyone should know about him. He was very, very big. Nobody knows exactly how big he was. But there *are* some stories. . . .

They say that when he was a baby, Paul was too big to stay in the house. So his father had to cut down tall trees to make a boat. His mother made a blanket as big as a football field. Then they put the boat on a river and tucked in Paul. The waves rocked him to sleep.

6

But in a lot of ways Paul was like any other baby. When he woke up, he wanted to play. He laughed. He rolled around in his boat bed.

And when Paul rolled, the boat made a wave taller than a house. Then it made a wave taller than two houses. The waves smashed onto the shore.

People on the land had to climb onto the roofs of their houses. They went up into trees. Some of them climbed up the church steeple.

After that, Paul's mother and father were more careful. As he grew up, they taught him many things. They had to tell him, "Don't step on farms. Don't lean on small mountains." They also taught him to use an ax. And that was what Paul really loved.

There were lots of trees to cut down in those days. America was covered with forests. People needed trees to make houses and farms and to help build railroads.

Nobody could cut down trees like Paul Bunyan. He would swing his shiny ax, and trees fell like toothpicks. He could cut down a whole forest before lunch and another one before dinner.

Paul liked his life as a logger. But he needed a friend. He was lonely for someone his own size.

Then came the Winter of the Blue Snow.

That winter, snow fell all over the land. The snow was as blue as the sky. No, it was bluer than that. It was as blue as blue ink. It came down in big, blue flakes. Nobody had ever seen anything like it.

One day, Paul was out walking in the blue snow. He was being very careful not to step on the snow-covered trees. And then he saw a small, blue mountain that he hadn't seen before. As he got closer, the mountain moved. Snow started to fall from the mountain. Paul saw two huge horns.

The mountain turned out to be an ox as blue as the snow and almost as big as Paul. Paul named the ox Babe. Babe the Blue Ox stayed with Paul all of his life and was his best friend.

Once Paul measured from one of Babe's eyes to the other. They were exactly twenty-seven ax handles and a plug of tobacco apart. Just one of Babe's iron shoes was so heavy that a man who tried to carry it would sink into the ground all the way up to his belt. If Paul could cut down a forest in one morning, then Babe could carry it on his back.

When Paul grew up, he had his own logging camp. He had a bookkeeper, named Johnny Inkslinger, and two cooks, named Sourdough Sam and Hot Biscuit Slim. And he hired hundreds of loggers. One was named Hals Halvorsen. He was almost as big as Paul.

Sourdough Sam and Hot Biscuit Slim used a griddle as big as an ice-skating rink. Every time they wanted to grease it, a dozen loggers strapped big chunks of bacon to their feet and skated on it until it was ready. Then the cooks would mix up a few hundred tons of pancake batter. When they poured it on the griddle, pancakes could be smelled from the Great Lakes to the Rocky Mountains. The cooks always made an extra train carload for Babe.

19

One of Paul's biggest jobs was in North Dakota. Back then, there wasn't an inch of land in North Dakota that wasn't covered with trees. And people wanted farms. So Paul said that he would clear the whole state. He made the biggest logging camp that the world has ever seen.

Every building in the camp was as big as a town. The dining room was so big that the loggers would get hungry just waiting in line for their food. So Paul built lunch counters every mile or so. That way, the loggers could have snacks while they were waiting for their meals.

Paul and Babe carried water to the camp from the Great Lakes. Paul put a big tank on Babe's back and filled it. As Babe walked to North Dakota, his hoofprints made holes in the ground. The water splashing from the tank filled the holes. That's why there are so many lakes in Minnesota. Once, Babe tripped. All of the water spilled from the tank and started the Mississippi River.

It didn't take long for Paul and Hals and the other loggers to cut down all of the trees in North Dakota. But then there was a problem. There were tree stumps every few feet across the entire state. Farms can't have tree stumps on the land!

"Hals," Paul said to his friend, "you and I have some work to do." The two of them walked all over the state of North Dakota. Every time they saw a tree stump, they used their big fists to pound it into the ground. In a week, they had pounded down every single stump.

Paul wanted to find out just how good the land was for farming. So he planted a kernel of corn. Before he could turn around and walk away, the corn started growing. It grew so fast that pretty soon the top of the stalk couldn't be seen.

"Hals," said Paul, "you climb up that cornstalk and cut off the top so it won't poke a hole in the sky." Well, Hals started climbing. But the corn was growing faster than Hals could climb.

In just a minute, Hals was out of sight, too. Paul yelled at him to come down. It took an hour for Hals's voice to reach the ground. "I'm trying. But the corn's going up faster than I can come down. And I'm getting hungry."

So Paul loaded a big shotgun with biscuits and shot them to Hals so that he wouldn't starve to death. And then Paul grabbed a bunch of rails from the logging railroad and tied them around the cornstalk as if he were tying a ribbon. The stalk kept on growing taller and wider, but the rails cut into it. In a few minutes, the cornstalk cut itself in half where the rails were tied.

The stalk was so tall that it took three days for all of it to fall. When it got close to the ground, Hals jumped off. "Well,"said Paul, "I guess the land is good enough for the farmers. So I'm finished here."

Paul said good-bye to all of his friends in the camp and started off to look for more trees to cut. He took Babe with him.

Once, as they were walking, Paul was careless. He let his ax drag behind him, and it dug out the ground to form the Grand Canyon.

When Paul was in California, he chopped down redwood trees. They were really big in those days. In fact, it used to rain every time a cloud bumped into a redwood.

Some people say Paul and Babe ended up in Alaska. Maybe they did. If so, Paul probably still swings his big ax. And Babe is walking right beside him.